Buddhism For Beginners

The Basic Understanding Of Fundamental Buddhist Teachings, Concepts, And Practices

Garland P. Brackins

Buddhism For Beginners

Description

The Buddhist philosophy is ancient and powerful. Its influence on the world, as we know it, is immeasurable. The Buddha taught that through his doctrine, the true nature of reality can be known and transcended. If you wish to unlock the mysteries of the mind and walk a balanced path to liberation, this book has found you for that reason exactly. In this book you will discover:

- The history of Buddhism
- Who the Buddha was during his life
- The Buddhist philosophy
- Meditation techniques
- The nature of reality
- How Buddhism thrives in modern times
- The path to liberation
- The science and Buddhism connection

Buddhism For Beginners

This book holds the key to beginning a Buddhist practice. If you have been curious about Buddhism or about the nature of life itself, then purchase this book now!

Buddhism For Beginners

Bluesource And Friends

This book is brought to you by Bluesource And Friends, a happy book publishing company.

Our motto is **"Happiness Within Pages"**
We promise to deliver amazing value to readers with our books.
We also appreciate honest book reviews from our readers.

Connect with us on our Facebook page www.facebook.com/bluesourceandfriends and stay tuned to our latest book promotions and free giveaways.

Don't forget to claim your FREE books!

Brain Teasers:

https://tinyurl.com/karenbrainteasers

Harry Potter Trivia:

https://tinyurl.com/wizardworldtrivia

Sherlock Puzzle Book (Volume 2)

https://tinyurl.com/Sherlockpuzzlebook2

Also check out our best seller book
"67 Lateral Thinking Puzzles"
https://tinyurl.com/thinkingandriddles

Table of Contents

Introduction

Chapter 1: What Is Buddhism?

    The Four Noble Truths

    Early History

    Growth of Buddhism in India

    Fractured Buddhism

    Expansion Throughout Asia

    Silk Road Expansion

Chapter 2: Buddha's Life and Teachings

Chapter 3: Empathy and Compassion

Chapter 4: Suffering

Chapter 5: Karma

    Origins

Chapter 6: Reincarnation

Chapter 7: Nirvana

Chapter 8: Enlightenment

Chapter 9: Meditation

    Types of Meditation

Buddhism For Beginners

Practice

    Day One

    Day Two

    Day Three

    Day Four

    Day Five

Chapter 10: Ritual, Prayer, and Offerings

    Ritual

    Prayer

    Offerings

Chapter 11: Buddhism and Modern Life

Conclusion

Introduction

Congratulations on downloading Buddhism for Beginners: The Basic Understanding of Fundamental Buddhist Teachings, Concepts, and Practices and thank you for doing so.

The following chapters will cover the basic concepts of Buddhism, its history, and practice. As one of the world's largest and most practiced religions, Buddhism has been adopted into many different cultures. Having originated in India centuries ago, the Buddhist philosophy and practice has traveled to all corners of the world, with dedicated followers and casual ones alike. Many of the Buddhist traditions such as meditational practice and adhering to the idea of reincarnation are well-established in the minds of many people around the world who wouldn't

Buddhism For Beginners

particularly consider themselves Buddhists. So what makes a practicing Buddhist a dedicated practitioner?

There are many different types of Buddhism that are considered proper traditions; Theravada, Mahayana, and Vajrayana are among the main three most popular traditions. These schools are also often divided into subdivisions as well. Unlike many other popular religions, there are many different sects and groups that consider themselves Buddhist. These various groups hold different opinions on the Buddha's teachings and are even known to feud amongst themselves over differing opinions. We will touch on the different traditions in this book, but overall, we want to focus on the general overview and basic principles that the Buddha has taught.

The following chapters will cover the history and influence of Buddhism, the basic principles of

Buddhism For Beginners

Buddhism, meditation, prayer, rituals, and other concepts that are found in the majority of Buddhist traditions.

There are plenty of books on this subject on the market so thanks again for choosing this one! Every effort was made to ensure that it is full of as much useful information as possible for the beginning student of Buddhist philosophy and practice.

Chapter 1: What Is Buddhism?

Buddhism stands as one of the most widely practiced religions in the modern world. The religion boasts over 500 million followers that adhere to the traditional teachings of Gautama Buddha, or simply named the Buddha. These teachings, founded in India, aim to overcome the worldly experience of suffering and overcoming the post mortem cycle of reincarnation through practices and dedication during the adherent's waking life. By living a righteous life and developing a dedicated practice based on the Buddha's teachings, the student aims to attain Nirvana, which liberates them from constant suffering and breaks the cycle of life, death, and rebirth, allowing them to leave behind earthly troubles and the problems of human life. The idea that humans overwhelmingly wish to hold on to impermanent things is called dukkha, loosely translated as 'incapable of experiencing fulfillment.' This lack of satisfaction creates an endless cycle of constantly repeated rebirth, also known as samsara, onto Earth unless we attempt to break away from the cycle through Buddhist practices and liberation. Attaining the nirvana state is attributed to following the Noble Eightfold Path.

With the lack of a proper god-like figure or metaphysical assumptions in the Buddha's teachings, Buddhism relies on a more philosophical truth than worship and adherence to a powerful being outside the sphere of humanity. Although we find influence of astrology, spirits, and subtle influences from a variety of other philosophies, these were not of concern to the Buddha. Even without the assistance of a god or speculative ideologies, Buddhism is built upon an unshakeable moral code.

The Four Noble Truths

Among the most important and popular philosophies, the four noble truths stand consistent in the majority of Buddhist schools. These truths are as follows:

- 'All life is suffering.' This train of thought is understood within the idea that something considered good is impermanent. Pain arises from the usual suspects such as death, illness, and abuse, but also from the idea that happiness is fleeting. The temporary nature of pleasure and joy is inevitably going to lead to longing and lack of satisfaction.

- 'The cause of all suffering is desire.' The thirst for pleasure and happiness always leads to suffering. Since the pleasure is inevitably going to end, suffering is sure to follow. Our intense human desires will always exhaust our resources thus leaving us in pain. Selfish desires are thought to be the extreme example of this, whereas selfless desires have the potential to not end in suffering.

- 'Ending desire will end suffering.' By not getting attached to earthly, material things or people, we can avoid the pain that comes along with the dramatic change. Since we, as we know ourselves, will eventually die and decay, then any attachment we have will be troublesome. Acknowledging this natural cycle and avoiding attachment, we can overcome suffering.

- 'Following the Eightfold Path ends desire.' The Eightfold Path is comprised of eight moral rules that are considered right or morally adjunct. These eight insightful rules include: right intentions, right action, right views, right speech, right livelihood, right effort, right concentration, and right mindfulness. These 'right' ways of behaving are akin to commandments in Christianity, although not as specific.

Along with these four truths and eight rules of behaving, we need to mention that there is no sin in Buddhism. In place of sin being the cause of suffering, the Buddha taught that ignorance was the ultimate source of suffering. Hand in hand with this thought is the lack of faith or belief in Buddhism. To overcome ignorance, you need understanding, and faith requires lack of evidence to support your understanding, therefore faith is not enough to overcome ignorance. This leads us to assume that this is why Buddhism requires no godhead to attain its ultimate goal. This is curiously affirmed by some Buddhist schools with the practice of assuming the

Buddha as a man who did not even exist, thus relieving the student of any desire to idolize the Buddha himself, and focus on his teachings.

These ideas that earthly existence is full of consistent suffering, pain, and impermanent states are the basis of Buddhist thought. Breaking away and seeing through the impermanence of existence on Earth is the ultimate goal, and is thought to allow the student to attain a new state of existence beyond earthly desires and needs. Earth as a vessel of desires that cannot be satisfied is an ancient thought process with its roots in the iron age of Indian life.

Early History

During the first millennium BCE, India was experiencing an intensive amount of social change. India's most influential texts, the Vedas, were not only being challenged by outside influences and thought, but even within the Vedic traditions. There were new philosophies arising and molding the schools of thought that had been popular for so long. Within the Vedic school of thought, Upanishads, thought to be the final chapters of the Vedas, arose and new ideas developed some challenging long held traditions. Outside of the Vedic thought rose Samsara movements. These movements found theirt origins in cultures and groups of people that renounced the earthly experience and thus challenged and rejected Vedic teachings. This renunciation of conventional society and traditional beliefs built many schools of thought, among them the Charvaka school, Jainism, and Buddhism.

During this time of dramatic social change, the Buddha lived and contributed to the challenging of the status quo. After his passing away, a community gradually grew as followers of his teachings created a religious-like movement that soon became known as

Buddhism. It seems that the religion of Buddhism was relatively humble compared to today, with such a small amount of historical evidence and written evidence. It is hard for scholars to know how popular the Buddhist way of thought actually was. Most agree that while the Buddha was alive, his teachings were mostly unknown except for a small group of followers who would carry on his teachings as they grew and evolved over time. While the Sramana religions were vastly practiced during pre-Buddha India, the philosophies and teachings remain a crucial aspect of the Buddhist traditions to this day.

Growth of Buddhism in India

As the earthly renunciation, religions became more popular, and the Vedas faded and were left to purists. Buddhism sees its rise to the top of popular religious practices. In the 3rd century BCE, Indian emperor, Ashoka the Great, announced Buddhism as the official state religion. He perpetuated the ideas and practices of Buddhism to such an extent that Buddhist monks were consulted for political decision-making. This encouragement of Buddhist thought made for an abundant amount archaeological evidence for the practice of Buddhism during and after Ashoka's reign. The timeframe between the Buddha's death and Ashoka's leadership wields very little evidence for Buddhism, aside from oral tradition.

The increase in practice and popularity of Buddhism is thought to be the firm foundation that contemporary Buddhism is built upon. Naturally, as the religion grew, many sects and different schools were founded, fracturing the religion as a whole, and spreading the different schools of thought around India as various adherents chose their preferred school and promoted its thought processes accordingly.

Fractured Buddhism

As with many religions, Buddhist groups have disagreements about the original doctrine taught by the Buddha. It is thought that even the first Buddhist council held soon after the Buddha's death was fraught with differing opinions and arguments over where the religion should be heading. Buddhist communities were formed in many different regions, and the wide range of languages used along with outside influences from other philosophies and religions resulted in distinct differences among the sects. With no universal authority and many leaders teaching different practices and doctrines, Buddhism finds itself spread thin over a very diverse and complicated land.

By the time the Second Buddhist Council was held, almost one hundred years after the Buddha's death, it is recorded that there were eighteen schools of early

Buddhist thought. This number is debatable, but generally speaking, there is thought to be twenty to twenty-five major schools at the time. One notable school that stands out during this schism is the Mahasanghika school. This school of thought was said to have broken away from the older traditions because of monastic practices. Other schools accused the Mahasanghika school of teaching that the Buddha had God-like attributes, contradicting the original school of thought. This main schism formed two main schools: the Mahasanghika and the Sthaviravada.

Expansion Throughout Asia

These two main schools of early Buddhism stood the test of time for a long while, seeing through many transformations, and broke off into a variety of sects and schools. Theravada school of thought rose in popularity stemming from the Sthaviravada school of thought. The Theravada line still exists today and is amongst the most popular in modern times. The Mahasanhika line eventually perished as an official mode of Buddhist thought. In south India, a school named Mahayana came to fruition as a more adaptable and easily accessible form of the religion. This school remains popular in Japan, Tibet, and China.

As trade routes became more and more open throughout Asia, merchants brought their religious views with them, spreading their worldviews and philosophies as vast as their goods and services. The religion traveled throughout Asia, reaching royalty and common people alike. As these trade routes made available access to the Buddhist thought, the mythology of the Buddha himself grew and transformed. By way of Sri Lanka, notably Sri Lankan royalty, Buddhism entered Myanmar, and it was said that the Buddha had traveled there and personally taught his way of life to the residents—this is now known to be false since it doesn't adhere to the archaeological timeline. From here, the religion traveled through Cambodia, Thailand, and Laos. Archaeological evidence supports Buddhism's arrival in Indonesia in the 5th century CE.

As Buddhism spread from its origins in India, Muslim invasions and the growth in popularity of Hinduism caused its popularity to dwindle in its homeland. Hindu practices even adopted some Buddhist philosophy, incorporating the Buddha himself in its large array of gods and goddesses.

Silk Road Expansion

During the Han dynasty in China, Buddhism entered via the Silk Road in the first century. Missionaries brought their philosophies and goods into China only to be met with long-held Chinese beliefs, comprised of ancient intellectual and technological superiority that China was so well-known for. The teachings of Confucius dominated the ruling class and saw Buddhism as unproductive and lackluster in its ability to be utilized in such an advanced civilization.

Having been met with such adversity, Buddhism still managed to build a solid foundation in China. As imperialism started to falter during the Six Dynasties era, foreign ideas were more openly accepted and began to meld with the Confucian dominated ideas. From China, Buddhism enters Korea and most notably Tibet, where we see it grow very powerful, but alas, sandwiched between two powerhouse countries like India and China, creating a lot of drama and tension.

Chapter 2: Buddha's Life and Teachings

The historical realities of the living Buddha have been debated amongst contemporary scholars for decades. Gautama Buddha, Siddhartha Gautama, and Siddhattha Gotama are all titles attributed to the man that became known as the Buddha. He taught a philosophy that became Buddhism, as we know it, and was thought to have lived during the 6th and 4th centuries BCE. Buddhists believe that this man was a truly enlightened teacher whose insights and lessons were profound and a powerful tool to attain an enlightened state. His goal to end suffering for sentient beings on Earth remains a mission for all Buddhists to this day. The Buddha's life and teachings are said to have been recorded by his followers soon after his death. Through oral traditions and eventually writings, his legacy and philosophies remain a crucial aspect of cultures all around the world today.

While historical facts about the Buddha cannot be a hundred percent verified, most practitioners of Buddhism uphold the belief that he was a man who taught and lived in India and even started a monastic order around 550-500 BCE. His story is typically told within a symbolic sequence, not unlike the very goals that adherents today try to attain. The sequence of birth, maturity, renunciation of the world, searching, liberation, teachings, and eventual death are generally accepted as the actual sequence of events that took place during his life. The timeline of his actual life is debatable among historians, but the majority of scholars agree that he was a living being and his teachings were his own.

There is a variety of resources when we reference the historical value of the Buddha's biography. While

Buddhism For Beginners

Buddhists in ancient India were more concerned with the philosophy than whether or not he was an actual man, today, we see a lot of focus on historical accuracy to validate the religion. The abundant amount of old texts and images that reference the living Buddha are often conflicting. The earliest known full biography is a poem attributed to the poet Asvaghosa in the 1st century CE. Newer resources vary in distinction and parallels, some with miraculous accounts of his descent from heaven and others free of any miracles or superhuman qualities.

Early depictions of the Buddha's biography do not attribute any super natural powers to the Buddha. These god-like attributes are typically found in later biographies. The Buddha's disciples agreed that he never claimed to have been simply a man or a god, but only possessed higher knowledge through his work renouncing worldly desires. His life as a Sramana is favored among some adherents claiming him not an antagonist to the Vedic tradition but as a reformer of Sramana beliefs. With all the different sects and traditions of the Buddha's biography, there are many that contain miraculous occurrences, from immaculate conception to his ability to sustain himself without food or drink. These traditional sources are still upheld in Buddhist circles while Western influence on these stories attempt to find a fitting biography free of the deified Buddha. While conflicting beliefs about his actual life on Earth are still held by Buddhists, it is generally accepted that he did possess a certain ability to be unaffected by worldly problems and to share his abilities as a teacher and sage.

While we do not have a historically sound be-all and end-all biography of the Buddha, we can be reasonably sure he was an actual historical figure with or without supernatural prowess. His accepted biography is as follows, give or take some exact details.

Gautama is born to a Hindu family, sometimes thought to be royalty, but in the very least, he is born a son of an elected official. His mother, Maya, was said to be a princess thus giving him a relatively favorable position in life. Maya claims that she dreamt of his birth, and that one night, a white elephant entered her on the right side. Ten months later, Siddhartha was born in his mother's kingdom, or at the least on their way to the kingdom. Some traditions state that Maya dies giving birth or days later. Siddhartha's birth is a celebrated one, with hermits and seers traveling from distant places to claim that he would become a great king. It is also thought that Siddhartha had distinct birth marks that verified the seer's claims.

Buddhism For Beginners

With his mother deceased, it is thought that Siddhartha was raised by his mother's sister. As per tradition for a newborn prince, he was raised in a royal household with three palaces built specifically for him. His father sheltered him from religious teachings and even went so far as to keep him from experiencing the outside world, so as to avoid any contact with the suffering of humans. Siddhartha was arranged to be married when he was 16, to a cousin of the same age. Some traditions even state that they birthed a son. It is said that Siddhartha lived 29 years, thriving in his royal lifestyle before his renunciation of the world.

At the age of 29, Siddhartha leaves his palace for the first time in efforts to meet the subjects of his court. This being against his father's wishes to shelter him, Siddhartha still sets out on his journey. Siddhartha meets an old man and soon learns for the first time that all people grow old. Upon this revelation, he is troubled and sets out on other adventures beyond the palace. These journeys are eye-opening to Siddhartha as he stumbles upon a decaying corpse, a disease-ridden man, and a man who has chosen to live a life free of pleasure, also known as an ascetic. These experiences depress Siddhartha, and he announces his goal to overcome the suffering of existence and decides to live a life like the ascetic.

Joined by his companion Channa and his loyal horse, Kanthaka, Siddhartha leaves his place in the royal palace. He sneaks out of his home without letting his family know, even sneaking passed the guards in the night. He leaves to Rajagaha and begins his ascetic life begging for sustenance in the street. Soon, the king and his men realize that Siddhartha is missing and in return offers him the throne. Siddhartha, dedicated to overcoming worldly suffering, kindly declines but promises to return to the kingdom once he attains his goals.

Buddhism For Beginners

Siddhartha continues his journey, studying under yogic teachers to learn meditation techniques to further his ascetic journey. When one teacher asks Siddhartha to succeed him, Siddhartha respectively declines and decides to learn under another teacher. Under this teacher, he attains very advanced levels of meditative skills. He is again asked to succeed his teacher but is unfulfilled with the thought of the yogic life and moves on with his journey.

Realizing that the ascetic life is not enough to reach his goals, he dedicates his time to meditation, soon realizing that the truest sense of being, or the middle way, is attainable through meditation. The middle way is a path dedicated to moderation, far from the extreme asceticism he had been practicing. Through this realization, he develops the Noble Eightfold Path. This realization leads Siddhartha to seat himself beneath a pipal tree and never leave his seat until he attains his goals.

Having aged to 35 years old, and notably losing a few followers, it is said that after 49 days of meditation, Siddhartha finally attains enlightenment. This is the moment he becomes known as the Buddha or 'enlightened' one. This is also the moment he realizes the Four Noble Truths, attaining liberation from amsara. The Buddha finds Nirvana, or extinguishes his desires, thus detaching from ignorance and breaking the cycle of reincarnation. Soon, Siddhartha has to decide whether or not to teach his philosophy and practice to others. He is convinced to do so by Brahma Sahampati, who argues that at least one person will understand and pursue the path of enlightenment.

Soon, the Buddha sets out to spread his teachings. He travels to northern India where he gives his first sermon to five companions who then join him on his teaching journey. Within months, he has dozens of adherents, with more to come in following months, thought grow to over a thousand. It is said that for the next 45 years, the Buddha travels teaching people from all walks of life: nobleman, servants, and even criminals.

Hearing of his son's enlightenment, the Buddha's royal father sends out groups of men to invite the Buddha back to his home. Nine of the groups fail to deliver the news before joining the Buddha's followers. The tenth succeeds, and the Buddha agrees to return to the palace. Upon arrival and subsequent meals and celebration, many of the members of the palace join the Buddha's disciples. It is famously reputed that Siddhartha is reluctant to teach women, but his foster mother would not accept this close-minded attitude and forms a group that followed the

Buddhism For Beginners

Buddha and his disciples until finally he is convinced to ordain females.

At the age of 80, the Buddha announces that it is time to leave his worldly body willingly. Nearing the deathless state, he eats his last meal, then becoming deathly ill, he spends his final moments among his followers. He offers to answer any final questions his disciples have, of which there are none. His final words are reported to be: "All composite things are perishable. Strive for your own liberation with diligence." It is also said that he instructs his disciples to follow no leader, though the disciples still form a Buddhist council with a chairman to keep the philosophy organized and to further the teachings of their beloved leader. The Buddha's body is cremated and some of his relics are said to survive today.

Chapter 3: Empathy and Compassion

At the core of the Buddhist philosophy is a sense of respect and loving kindness toward all sentient things. As we learned from the history of the Buddha, he set out to share his teachings with the world in efforts to rid the people of earth of their suffering. This is no small feat and requires an immense amount of empathy and compassion toward his fellow man and the other sentient creatures of earth. Through contemplative and meditational practice, the Buddha found that he could transverse the worldly attachments that created all suffering. These practices most certainly included contemplation on an empathetic and compassionate attitude toward all sentient beings. But what is empathy and compassion? And are they absolutely necessary for a Buddhist practice?

All sentient beings experience suffering as a constant and intrusive state of pain or discomfort. Although there may be times when we can seem to escape the suffering, it always returns as our pleasure dissipates. Exhausting resources that create pleasure is inevitable, thus leaving a feeling of longing and dissatisfaction. When we see others experiencing this pain, we tend to feel for them or wish to help in some way. By focusing on reducing the suffering of others, we help ourselves learn the true nature of suffering and can better understand these ancient concepts. Through contemplating suffering or focusing our intention on empathy and compassion, we train ourselves to feel for others and feel for ourselves. The Buddha had much to say about these states of emotion, but let's define the terms first.

Empathy and compassion are often mistaken as synonyms. Although they go hand-in-hand, they are quite different. Empathy can be defined as the action and ability to share and understand another sentient being's feelings. Compassion is defined as sympathy, pity, and true concern for the suffering of other sentient beings. In Buddhism, the practice of compassion is called karuna. The practice aims to attain an active compassion for people who are obviously suffering, but also to keep a consistent compassion for all sentient beings since they are stuck in a cycle of suffering. While being empathetic and sharing other's feelings can be useful, it can also be draining to experience too much empathy, and here, compassion comes into play. By immersing yourself in a compassionate attitude at all times, you are motivated to assist in the releasing other beings from their suffering. While most people naturally have compassion for others, we can also practice compassionate contemplation for others. We also need to be careful not to wish others to be well in search of fulfilling our own desires. If we have a loved one who is in pain and we wish them to be relieved because we need something from them, whether it's their presence or insight, we are using compassion for selfish reasons. This is essentially attachment rising up through our attempt to be compassionate.

There have been scientific studies on the different effects of empathy and compassion on the brain. Studies affirm what the Buddha believed about the value of compassion versus empathy. They show that empathy can have detrimental effects on the mind of the empathetic person. This leads us to know that empathy can cause an exhausting feeling, almost like an empathy burnout when used over and over again. On the other hand, studies show that compassion and altruistic kindness actually have the opposite effect, reinforcing love and positive attitudes while not leading to any exhausting effects. By being selfless and loving, the human perspective does not get exhausted, but in fact, helps the compassionate person and the sufferer to surmount negative feelings.

When practicing compassionate meditation as a Buddhist, one may reflect on the sufferings of all beings, picturing the atrocities of the world that harm all beings. This intensive practice can be done to the point that it becomes unbearable to the practitioner. By placing ourselves in this state, we develop an understanding of suffering that motivates us to work to help release suffering for all beings. The natural desire to help is often not enough to motivate one to work to relieve suffering, so by experiencing intensive suffering and learning the nature of the pain, we develop a determination to work to end the cycle. Reflecting on the source of suffering, ignorance, and attachment, we increase our power to achieve relief and help others to do so as well.

Buddhism For Beginners

By contemplating compassion and how we wish to use it, we can train ourselves to be compassionate in a selfless way—this is the compassion of the Buddha state. We can train ourselves to cherish other sentient beings and wish them to be released from their suffering. Even if our immediate loved ones are seemingly having a good day, we can still use compassion focused on them knowing that the pleasure is fleeting. These practices work on many levels, often viewed as a limited individual compassion and a universal compassion that you exist within for all living beings.

If we wish to be compassionate toward others, we can meditate on them, picture them in your mind being filled with golden light and physically view the suffering leaving them. Doing this during a meditation, practice can be very beneficial for you and your immediate loved ones, but don't stop there. Focus on people you don't even know and even the

Earth itself being released of the cycle of pain and suffering.

In conclusion, we find that it's important to learn the difference between compassion and empathy. Empathy is the ability to share another's pain, whereas compassion is more sympathetic and active immersion in the suffering of an individual or even the entire world. Empathy can be exhausting and detrimental; compassion is constructive and even reinforces the desire to be selfless and loving toward all sentient beings. By learning to be compassionate at all times and deepening our understanding of suffering, we better prepare ourselves for an enlightened state. Here, we learn that karuna, or compassion, is a crucial aspect of the original mission statement that the Buddha set out to complete.

Chapter 4: Suffering

As we learned from Buddha's teachings, suffering is an inevitable constant attached to existence. Defined as a state of distress or pain, suffering is the ultimate hardship that encompasses all distress and discomfort. As Buddha taught, all desire for impermanent things such as immortality or material possessions are eventually going to lead to suffering. This attachment to something impermanent creates pleasure but a pleasure that is soon vanished due to the lack of perpetual resources to maintain the pleasure state. So, in turn, the desire for these things is a result of ignorance of the true nature of pleasure and pain. This true nature of all existence is called dukkha in Buddhist thought.

Buddhism For Beginners

In our contemporary society, suffering is often hidden from sight, being ignored or hidden from plain sight. This suppression of pain is a feeble attempt by our society to avoid dealing with uncomfortable things and indulge in only pleasurable experiences. Death is not discussed among families, sickness is not viewed as an inevitable aspect of existence, and pain is not a topic of discussion for children and young adults. This avoidance of distress only creates more attachment to the pleasures of worldly life. If we avoid pain and do not acknowledge its role in existence, then we are focusing all of our energy and attention on our superficial attachments, thus strengthening our ties to the earthly realm and supporting our entrapment in the cycle of reincarnation.

The Buddha taught practices that aimed to end suffering, but how is this possible since we are caught up in the vicious cycle? One first great step is to not deny or ignore pain and suffering. We must embrace the discomfort even in the most extreme cases. By opening our hearts to the fact that suffering is a crucial and unavoidable aspect of life, we find that heart's capacity to handle the painful aspects of awareness is immense. We learn that it is not the suffering itself that is detrimental, but our reaction to the suffering where we find ourselves feeling lost and alone.

When we learn that we are capable of using suffering against itself, we acquire the confidence to reach out and touch an important truth about existence—that suffering is just another natural part of the grand scheme of things. It is not separate from pleasure but goes hand in hand. For instance, how would we know we are suffering if we have never felt pleasure and vice versa? This realization when it comes to fruition, induces a very comforting and peaceful state. By replacing the societal standard of denying pain with compassion and awareness of its role, we can make great progress towards the attainment of enlightenment.

While the realization of the inescapable nature of suffering is liberating, it is not going to completely end suffering. There is no magical solution that is going to end pain, but the acceptance of suffering will help you to develop ways of coping with loss, death, and illness. By accepting suffering as an integral role in existence, we find ourselves content with its sudden intrusions into our lives. It simply is. This is dukkha. Do not develop huge expectations pertaining to the ultimate solution of suffering; it doesn't exist here on our earthly plane. Instead, be accepting of the distress, and realize it is inevitable and unavoidable. This being said, we must also not just sit around wallowing in pain.

Buddhism For Beginners

The Buddha taught that we must actively engage in the reduction of the suffering of others. There are many ways to go about this. Compassion, as mentioned above, goes a long way to reduce suffering of other sentient beings. Also, let's not take for granted the day-to-day things we do that reduce suffering in others. The parent that ensures their children are well-fed and healthy. The pet lover that adopts and nurtures animals, giving them food and a great home. And even the keeping of plants or a garden goes a long way to directly and indirectly reduce suffering. These common aspects of human life that require attention and nurturing are incredible ways to reduce the suffering of others while also engaging yourself in activities that help you develop practices to reduce suffering. The key to these nurturing activities is recognizing that they are impermanent and to not let attachment to these other beings overtake you and create even more suffering. Recognize that everything will die and decay. This may seem morbid or negative, but indeed, it is necessary if we wish to reduce suffering in ourselves, and step closer to our ultimate goal of liberation and enlightenment.

As we contemplate the nature of suffering, we must keep a keen eye that we are not exhausting our emotional resources, that we have a healthy means of engaging with pain and working with it rather than against it to benefit ourselves and others. Since we cannot change our inevitable experience of pain, before or after the fact, we must become adept in the practice of acceptance. Accepting the fact that suffering is inescapable and can only be nullified through ignorance or denial is one of the foundational building blocks of the Buddha's teachings. Knowing that you are powerless to change the fact that life is suffering should not be a detrimental thought but an uplifting and liberating one. If you cannot avoid it, then something else must be done to deal with the distress and pain. Do not be disheartened by the lack of control you have over the true nature of things. Many people wish to have this incredible and nonexistent power, but alas, there is no feasible way to overcome suffering except through the breaking of the karmic cycle and leaving our earthly attachments behind.

Chapter 5: Karma

The idea of karma is one that has permeated many philosophies even outside of the Buddhist sphere of thinking. Karma is the idea that your decisions in any previous states of existence have a direct effect on your current life. So, if in a past life you were making terrible decisions, inflicting pain on others or yourself intentionally, then in this life, you will have unfavorable experiences. It also works the opposite way. If you were a righteous individual in a past life, helping others and being selfless, then you will be born into a favorable position in this current life and hopefully have a reliable beginning to further your good deeds throughout your current life, thus moving closer to enlightenment.

Buddhism For Beginners

Karmic concepts are found in Hindu beliefs as well, but we will focus strictly on the karma traditions practiced in Buddhism. In Sanskrit, karma is loosely translated to 'doing' or 'to take action.' The Buddhist belief being that any action you perform has a distinct consequence in the future, typically in another life but even sooner in the current life you live. The most common belief is that your actions will decide what you are born into in the next life after you're reincarnated. This concept is often described using a metaphorical image of fruit maturing as your karmic deeds are furthered.

So depending on your actions, whether good or bad, you influence your next life dramatically. By following the Eightfold Path and contemplating the Four Noble Truths, you have a set of guidelines that will only be favorable in your next life, or even allow you to attain enlightenment. With this in mind, we must mention that the Buddha taught that not everything in your current life is based on karmic reasoning. He felt that the process was much more fluid and susceptible to many other factors, but karma was still a very important concept.

The idea of rebirth and reincarnation is crucial when trying to understand karma. Most Buddhist traditions believe that there are six realms that birth and death exist within, and beings cycle through these realms living in ignorance and coveting desire forever, unless the being adheres to the Buddhist path to attain liberation. If one is successful on this path, then the attachment and desire is stopped and rebirth is stopped, breaking the cycle of reincarnation and liberating the individual. This cycle is driven by karma, or the individual's intention and action through speech, mind, and body. The development of this concept was very important to ancient philosophy. While most concepts stated that only certain people could attain an enlightened state, the idea of karma allowed anyone the access to liberation, not just royalty or certain demographics.

The idea and definition of intention is debated among the various schools of Buddhism, but for our goals in this book, we will define intention as what an individual aims to do, whether stated, allowed, or thought quietly to oneself. Good or 'right' moral behavior would accumulate over the course of a life and generate a favorable rebirth in the next realm. These are metaphorically considered to be seeds planted in the mind. The seeds are planted in one's life and can be nurtured in the next. This idea is great motivation for individuals to behave in a morally upstanding way. Why act cruelly when the repercussions are so vast? In fact, there are eternal repercussions for despicable behavior. The karmic debt you acquire is considered karmaphala, or 'fruits of you action.' This means that even despicable actions plant seeds that can ripen into a fruit in the next life, but surely this fruit is bitter and not as favorable as one planted with seeds of good deeds.

There is also the idea that disturbing experiences, those outside of your control, can plant unfavorable seeds. Some schools believe that, although you are not intending to plant unfavorable seeds, you can experience intense pain or sadness that can leave seeds behind and grow into bitter fruits on the next life. This leaves open a debate on the nature of intention. It seems that others can use their powerful intention to affect the seeds planted for future rebirths.

The karmic concepts and how intention affects rebirth is considered endless. So naturally, this brings up debate on the impermanence of rebirth. Many schools debate on how to reconcile this duality. In early Buddhist thought, there is no set theory on how rebirth and intention worked, but the idea that rebirth is caused by ignorance remains strong, perhaps ignorance of rebirth itself contributes to this cycle.

Many argue that karma is akin to fate or destiny, but this simply is not true. Some religions that adhere to the idea of fate claim that your fate is determined by a judgement, often by a powerful god or other being. This intensive judgement of your actions, as we can see, is quite different from your actions planting seeds for future lives. This can be simply explained: your experiences may be a result of past actions, but your reaction to your current experiences are not predetermined. How you react to your suffering in this life will, in turn, affect your rebirth in the next life.

The main point of the ideas of karma is to wholeheartedly recognize that the cycle exists. By acknowledging this cycle of birth, death, rebirth, and the influence of past intentions, we find that we create an internal dialogue with ourselves that questions our intentions as quickly as we can think of them. This contemplation of our intentions will allow us to question the morality of our actions. Are we making a 'right' decision? Will this decision reduce my suffering or the suffering of others? Does the decision adhere to the Eightfold Path? This internal dialogue is key to realizing the potential of planting seeds for future lives. Being compassionate and intending to reduce the suffering of the world as much as possible will certainly plant favorable seeds.

Origins

As mentioned above, the karmic philosophy broke through a biased philosophy that favored the rich and convinced other beings that they are lost to never being able to attain liberation from suffering. The original concept of karma is attributed to the Vedic religion; it was said that good deeds and ritual performance ensured the practitioners entrance into heaven. In Buddhism, before the fracturing into different schools, karma is thought to have been a minor and less important idea than contemporary Buddhism. Scholars believe that karma was lumped together with many other ideas on rebirth. Since the Buddha was mainly concerned with a 'deathless' state, the idea of rebirth may not have been presented until much later in his life. It is thought that physical actions and intentions do not affect rebirth, but mental and emotional ones are the most important when contemplating rebirth. There are dozens of differing opinions on the idea of influencing rebirth during waking life, but the important idea is that if you are choosing good actions, good consequences will come.

There are other ways to counter an unfavorable rebirth as well. In Tibetan Buddhism, it is believed that you can purify your negative seeds through meditational practices in this life. This would mean that if the proper action is taken, you can avoid any negative consequences of past lives' actions. This is often compared to Catholic confession among scholars, although the concepts are quite different.

In a modern Buddhism, there is much debate about external influences. We live in a world where popular culture may influence the individual's intentions negatively. Conditioned social norms and expected ways of living may not adhere to the karmic idea of planting well-intended seeds. How does one not contribute to an unfavorable rebirth if they are forced to work for a corporation that indirectly affects the environment in a terrible way? The debate on this eventually leads to call for action to reform the karma doctrine. Many believe that trying to accumulate favorable karmic value is selfish in itself and that intense focus on doing good things only to receive a favorable rebirth is detrimental to the individual. And, on the other hand, the karmic ideas may unintentionally cause people to be passive if they are faced with oppression from other groups. Let's say, someone causes you great harm, treats you unfairly, and is attempting to destroy your values and culture. Do you simply sit and take it to avoid any bad karma? Or do you fight back and potentially cause another being to suffer? This is a very conflicting attitude that many have debated.

In essence, your intention is the key. That internal dialogue should be exercised rigorously as you make decisions to plant favorable seeds for your future rebirths. Make decisions that empower yourself as an individual. It is safe to say that the action you take to enact karmic grace should not be used to justify racism, oppression, or to undermine other classes or religions. The Buddha certainly wouldn't want his students using karma to cast blame or justify accusing others of having bad karma. There is no just cause to claim you know about others' karma. Be humble and tread lightly when working with this concept.

Chapter 6: Reincarnation

Along with the ideas of rebirth and karma, we have the cycle of reincarnation. Loosely defined as the rebirth of an individual's soul into a new body, reincarnation is a crucial aspect of the Buddhist philosophy. As we have discussed, the Buddha taught that sentient beings are stuck in a cycle of birth, life, death, and rebirth. The rebirth aspect would be considered reincarnation. Pertaining to karma, the individual will be rebirthed into different bodies depending on how favorable the seeds hey planted in their past lives are.

The endless cycle of samsara and its painful nature, dukkha, is only broken by liberation by following the Buddhist path. This is the general idea, but reincarnation is much more complex and, much like karma, has evolved over time and even permeated other culture outside of the Buddhist sphere. There is often references to reincarnation peppered throughout popular Western culture. Often in jest, you may hear a character in a movie or TV show reference being reincarnated as an insect or something else considered gross in return for some negative behavior. This is in reference to the six realms, considered the extent of what a soul can be reincarnate into.

So being reborn is not just limited to being human. The other potential reincarnations include: the heavenly realm, the demigod realm, animal realm, ghost realm, and the realm called Naraka, which is synonymous with Hell. Although Buddhism claims there is no 'self,' there is thought to be a soul that transmigrates body to body, realm to realm, all depending on the amount of good or bad karma that the soul has accumulated over past lives. Obviously, some realms are considered evil or good, but depending on the perspective, all can be considered neutral since the main goal is to attain Nirvana. And so, the soul, rather than the material self, is continuing the journey. So, if your name is John or Jan in this life, that is yourself, your soul is not called John once you die. The soul can also be likened to consciousness. Some schools state that the soul migrates immediately after death, while others, such as Tibetan schools, believe there is a distinct amount of time between death and rebirth called bardo, and is said to last up to 49 days.

Some early texts state that the Buddha had a difficult time explaining rebirth after he claimed there is no self. If there is no self, then how do we travel body to body? One fitting analogy is that the soul is similar to a flame of a candle; it can be used to light another candle and transfer its nature and basic action. So the lack of self doesn't mean that that there is a lack of continuous experience. To reiterate, many believe that the Buddha was referencing the earthly and materialistic self when he claimed there to be no self. Some Buddhists even believe that there is a personal entity that keeps track of the karmic merit of a soul. This can be compared to a guardian angel or holy daimon found in other religions and occult texts. This personal entity concept caused a lot of feuding among various sects of Buddhism.

Buddhism For Beginners

Other schools claim that a soul will be reborn over and over until the karma has worked out all its consequences. With this idea, one could potentially be reborn over and over forever if they make no effort to reduce their karmic debt, and keep adding unfavorable debt to their karmic bill. Of the various rebirths, it is thought that certain attachments need to be released, starting with your personally identity, or self, and continuing to detach until you can effectively detach from ignorance itself. If you can attain the detachment from ignorance, it is said that you will not be reborn and can attain a Nirvana-like state.

With all of this in mind, it is important to consider how this cycle affects the earthly realm we thrive in. Ancient and modern Buddhists have argued that ghost experiences and near-death experience are material proof of rebirth. In many cultures, there are practices to induce a trance state that allows one to see into their past lives and potentially relive parts of it. These meditational states are thought to be higher perceptions of reality, and many attribute these experiences to reincarnation. There is much debate on the legitimacy on these ideas within the Buddhist community and outside of it in more materialist worldviews. Many of those in favor of these concepts hold dear the idea that there is no separation of the physical and the mental. By not separating these into different things and viewing them as one in the same, the ideas of rebirth have a bit more breathing room to form and be contemplated. Along with this idea is one where the mind cannot simply come from matter, i.e. the brain. This complex and thought-provoking dialogue is wonderful to contemplate with meditational practices.

The concept of reincarnation is crucial for the foundation of Buddhism. With the various realms and eternal cycle of suffering acting as a material trap, we have something to contrast a liberated state. Now that we have a firm grip on the nature of suffering and the cycles it creates, let's discuss this liberated state and its nature, one of which is even more complex, while at the same time being as simple as a breath.

Chapter 7: Nirvana

As we continue on our Buddhist journey, we need to take time to assess and contemplate the goals we aim to achieve. If enlightenment is the action of being liberated then Nirvana is the state of liberation we have achieved. This state is considered to be one of perfection; it is considered the highest form of true happiness and freedom. The Buddha taught that the most effective way to achieve this liberated state of freedom was to follow the Eightfold Path with meticulous fervor. This state is known to the adherent as soon as he or she realizes the true nature of non-self. Once the emptiness of non-self is realized, the practitioner is no longer trapped in samsara, or the endless cycle of death and rebirth.

Buddhism For Beginners

The Buddha taught that the state of Nirvana can be attained either during life or after death, depending on the karmic merits the student of Buddhism contributed during all their lives. Nirvana loosely translates in English to mean snuffed out. This often is miscommunicated as something negative when in fact it is referring to extinguishing the flames of desire. To eliminate your earthly attachments, rid yourself of anger, and see through your delusions you attain this transcendental state of bliss. Buddhist traditions also identify three fires or poisons that are attributed to earthly attachment: raga or greed, dvesha or hate, and avidya or ignorance. As we see, this state of bliss is closely linked with karma by accumulating positive karmic deeds, aiming to be compassionate toward others, and spending your time reducing the suffering of others. We plant the seeds that will fruit into favorable rebirths, hopefully leading to enlightenment and the state of Nirvana.

Buddhism For Beginners

The idea of Nirvana is found in many cultures and religions. Many scholars compare this blissful state to heaven in Christian and Vedic concepts, although a heavenly state is not commonly known to be attained until after death. In pre-Buddhist thought, the Vedas held strong onto the idea of heaven and hell, but many adherents found the concepts to be too simplistic for how complex the nature of the afterlife is. These challengers felt that a permanent hell or impermeable heaven was contradictory to the fluidity of existence itself. Soon, these troublesome concepts were somewhat fixed with the ideas of karmic merit and the cycle of life, death, and rebirth.

While the Buddha taught that nothing is permanent, it is suitable that he did not teach of a permanent hell or heaven, since this contradicts his ideas. He found that the two states of Nirvana, in life or after death, are attributed to the cessation of worldly things, completely detaching from everything, thus achieving an emptiness that shows the practitioner that there truly is no essence or fundamental nature of existence.

The concept on Nirvana seems very straightforward but in its truest form is a very complex and difficult state to achieve. Consider eliminating every attachment to everyone or everything in your life. In our modern and technology-advanced society, we value connection and attachment almost above anything else. Buddhists feel that this only strengthens our mental attachments and furthers our ignorance of the nature of existence. By creating incredibly strong ties to our material possessions and our loved ones, we only set ourselves up for more suffering, as the things we love are not permanent and will eventually disappear. Although, for many, the attainment of Nirvana, while still living, may not be possible, so perhaps it will be attained after. The student of Buddhism should be careful not to get discouraged by the difficulty of attaining a liberated state. Although we may not be able to completely eliminate suffering for ourselves and the world in this life, we can collect karmic merit by remaining compassionate and aiming to reduce suffering for other sentient beings.

The attainment of Nirvana is the ultimate goal of the Buddhist practitioner; this transcendental state of being is the utmost point of happiness and solitude. The Buddha stated that there were not any earthly words that could even begin to describe this state. For our cause here, we can use the closest words we have to try and describe the state—quiet, blissful, and potentially even beyond feeling anything at all. Although the idea of emptiness is often associated with lack of fulfillment in modern times, the Buddha felt that the emptiness he felt was the true state of non-being. This non-self is the core of the Buddhist doctrine; all our attachments and desires are delusions and distractions, which only thwart our true abilities to experience reality for what it is, empty and blissful.

Buddhism For Beginners

While the accumulation of wealth is coveted and celebrated in our world, it is good advice to contemplate these Buddhist ideals and take a step back from our intense desire to own things and have friends that need us. The balance of these two opposite ideas will provide the beginning student of Buddhism with great tools to further their success on the Buddhist path.

Chapter 8: Enlightenment

We have seen that Nirvana is the state of being liberated from the drudgery of samsara, or the cycle of life, death, and rebirth. Now, we need to discuss the action of becoming liberated itself, known as enlightenment. While enlightenment is most certainly an English term, its definition has its roots in Buddhism. Bodhi, or knowledge, is the Sanskrit word attributed to enlightenment or awakening. This action is thought to occur as soon as the practitioner attains a liberated state, whether during life or after death. What this moment feels like is difficult to describe, even for the Buddha, but much like Nirvana described above, enlightenment is the action of breaking the cycle of samsara and freeing yourself from suffering.

Buddhism For Beginners

The exact nature of the moment of enlightenment is relatively unknown, but a sense of freedom and quiet happiness is described. This moment is found when the student of Buddhism successfully walks the Eightfold Path and no longer finds themselves trapped by their desires and attachments to worldly experiences.

While the word 'enlightenment' has been adopted into the language of Western culture as a romanticized version of spiritual knowledge or higher learning faculties, the original meaning was much more impactful to the follower of the Buddhist path. Self-realization, acknowledgement of the true self, and revealing of the emptiness of existence accompany the enlightened moment. Many different schools of Buddhism exist and may have different word and definitions for this moment that the flame of desire is snuffed out, but overall, the majority of sects agree that this is canon in the Buddhist way.

Buddhism For Beginners

We have discussed the means of attaining this moment and subsequent state of Nirvana, and we will discuss the techniques and practices in later chapters. But to reiterate, maintaining compassion for others, aiming to reduce the suffering of other sentient beings, and acknowledgement of the emptiness of existence are all crucial realizations that need to be attended to achieve enlightenment.

Is there a way to know you have reached an enlightened state? It is hard to say. But as any Buddhist will tell you, you shouldn't even desire to be enlightened. This contradicts the whole point of selflessness. Take a moment to think about being enlightened. If you are truly enlightened, you certainly would not be worried about whether or not you are in fact enlightened. Contemplating this duality is a great exercise for the Buddhist mindset. Not having the desire to be enlightened may help lead to an enlightened state, but how do you go about achieving enlightenment if you do not desire it? This is a very challenging aspect of the Buddhist path. Overall, keep in mind that we are aiming to reduce suffering of the whole world and not simply trying to attain higher knowledge for ourselves and our selfish reasons. Keep this quote in mind:

"Anyone claiming to be enlightened certainly is not."

This short sentence will go a long way during contemplation, exercise, and also when you encounter teachers and other students on your journey.

The contradictory nature of eliminating desire is a complicated one. We desire to rid ourselves of desire. This duality can be contemplated for a lifetime, so it is best to not focus on what you wish to achieve through your Buddhist practice, and focus more of your energy on how you can reduce suffering for others. Always keep in mind that the Buddha was set on eliminating suffering for all other sentient beings, not just wanting to know the mysteries of life for himself. As we behave in selfless ways, we also find that our selflessness will benefit us, although we may not see it immediately. Forming habits that adhere to the Eightfold Path are only going got be beneficial for our ultimate goal of attaining enlightenment, whether we notice it or not. As one embraces a selfless lifestyle, it is not uncommon to feel as if we are selling ourselves short or acting in a detrimental way toward ourselves. This is directly attributed to our attachment to our own self-worth. Since we have spent the majority of our lives focused on building ourselves up and focusing on our own confidence, taking on a selfless view of the world may seem foreign at first, but with a little time and effort, we see the fruits of the selfless seeds we plant.

Buddhism For Beginners

This path to enlightenment is just that, a path. It may have twist and turns, sometimes be treacherous, and sometimes be comfortable. All along this path are personal challenges and those that need to be faced within groups and together with loved ones. By adhering to the Buddhist doctrine of the Eightfold Path and contemplation on the Four Noble Truths, we find ourselves adjusting naturally to a selfless lifestyle. Whether or not we attain enlightenment in this lifetime is certainly not a desire we need to hold on to. We need to detach from this thought and focus more of our efforts on the travelling of the path rather than the destination itself.

Chapter 9: Meditation

Meditation is one of the most important practices in Buddhism. Consider the Buddha siting beneath the tree for the 49 days before he attained his liberation from earthly suffering. The goal of meditation is to quiet the mind and train yourself to be in control of the chaotic and unorganized patterns that are constant in the human mind. By learning to achieve a sense of one-pointedness, you are your thoughts; you can better focus on what you wish to focus on and not be distracted by external stimuli. While the human mind is still very mysterious, even today with incredible technologies, meditation gives insight into the true nature of the mind and offers teachings about yourself as an individual.

In recent decades, meditation as a powerful practice has made its way from the East into the Western culture as a very effective means to find balance in a hectic and fast-paced society. Along with yoga and other Eastern concepts, meditation has influenced the Western mindset very positively and meaningfully. Today, even large businesses and corporations are promoting meditation for their employees to create a more relaxed atmosphere and improve their worker's attitude in the workspace. As a means of relaxation and overall health, meditation is very beneficial, and a dedicated practice can transform every aspect of your life in incredible ways. As a meditation practice is formed and adhered to, the student can learn to clear their mind and develop awareness beyond our natural day-to-day perception. This tends to alter consciousness and invoke deep thought about our perspective on the world we live in. With these valuable skills, anyone can calm themselves physically and emotionally. Studies have proven that meditation reduces anxiety and stress while also improving neurological health. With science and history on its side, meditation is a proven method to improve your overall well-being.

Meditation in an ancient practice that many religions use to attain higher knowledge and further their capabilities of devotion and one-pointedness. The word itself derives from the Latin word *meditari*, which means 'to think or ponder.' When trying to define meditation in modern terms, we find a wide range of definitions and meanings, but overall, when we reference meditation in the Buddhist sense, we are referring to deep thought and contemplation. This may seem pretty simple for such a profound practice, but many beginners come to find that calming the chaotic thought processes of the human mind is no small feat.

There are many different ways to induce a meditative state. Simply sitting and thinking about your day can be considered a meditative practice, which is an easy way to begin a meditational practice. There is a wide variety of techniques and practices to use to assist you in meditation: mala beads, chanting, breathing techniques, postures, and music are all excellent tools to use to enter into a meditative trance.

As we continue on, let's consider our goals with beginning a meditative practice. The Buddha taught that these ancient practices can allow the mind to experience a higher understanding of the nature of reality. To attain these experiences takes a very long time and a lot of dedication, so we will set our goals to be a little but easier. Sit and contemplate what you wish to achieve with your practice and keep this goal in mind before and after your practice.

Types of Meditation

For our modern understanding, there are two main forms of meditation: mindfulness meditation and concentrative meditation. Concentrative meditation involves voluntarily focusing on one object, typically an image or a sound. Mindfulness meditation involves a more passive approach, where the student is simply letting whatever thoughts that come to mind pass by. This technique is attempting to train the mind to not react to or follow any certain thoughts that come. Within these two definitions, there are almost infinite amounts of customization, and people tend to find what works best for them depending on what they are trying to achieve.

Practice

Once we have thought about what we aim to achieve through our newfound meditation process, we can begin our practice. Pick a certain time of the day that fits your schedule, and do your best to meditate during this time every time you meditate. You will also want to have a dedicated space where you can meditate without distraction. You also will find that this space will become homely and comfortable to you, and this will help you enter into a meditative state as you get used to the space being your meditation home. If you do not have an entire room, you can choose a corner or certain wall to face as your meditation home. Outdoor spaces are great too, but keep in mind the added distractions that are out of your control while outdoors.

Once you have your space picked out, you will want to decorate it and make it your own. Hang tapestries or other pleasing images—remember to pick a décor that is not going to distract you or cause you to lose your train of thought. Mandalas and pleasing patterns are great to use in your space and common among practitioners all around the world. An image or statue of the Buddha in a meditative position in space is also very common. This is not particularly for worship, but its acts as a reminder of the Buddha and his teachings. Incense, candles, stones, and other thought-provoking items are excellent additions to your meditation space. Make it your own special space; you want this space to be symbolic of you and your goals on the Buddhist path. Once you have your space nice and welcoming, you can begin planning your meditative practice. You obviously do not have to follow this guide exactly. There are infinite ways to find your meditative state, but for an easier explanation, we will lay out a five-day guide of 20-minute meditation sessions. This will be an easier approach for the beginner. Feel free to alter or customize the practice to make it your own.

Day One

As you start, you may want to turn down the lights, light some incense or candles, and get seated comfortably. Sit and let the thoughts come as they please. Try to not get caught up on any one thought or memory, just letting them flow by perhaps even picturing them leaving your mind. For your first session, breathe normally and really sink into you seat comfortably. You will want to have good posture during the session, keeping your back straight and making sure you're not going to harm yourself sitting in an awkward position for a long duration of time. As you are setting and letting the thoughts pass by, notice how you are feeling. What thoughts are coming? Is it easy for you to detach from the memories and thoughts? How does the room feel? Is your breath consistent? Asking yourself these questions will help you work on what aspects are holding you back from achieving a meditative state.

Buddhism For Beginners

Stay seated and focused for 20 minutes, and afterward, ask yourself the questions again and keep close attention to how you feel mentally and physically.

Day Two

For the second day, letting us be seated at the same time of the day is possible. Begin your session as you please with your chosen incense or candles. This day, we will add a simple breathing exercise to the session. Inhale slowly and deeply filling your lungs completely, holding the breath, count to three and exhale completely. Be sure to exhale all the air in your lungs, then repeat this breathing exercise for the duration of the session. It's okay if you cannot keep the breathing exercise consistent; it is common for beginners to get distracted or lose the rhythm of the breath. This breathing exercise not only helps you stay focused and not get caught up in thoughts, but will also help create a rhythm for the session. As you practice this exercise, it will become much easier to get in the 'zone' and synchronize the rhythm of your breathing to your practice. Finish your practice with the similar questions and observations from day one. These observations are going to help you develop your practice to achieve your goals.

Day Three

This day, we will add visualization to our session. Start the session as you have the past two days and get settled in and comfortable with your breathing. Once you've found a nice rhythm, start to visualize your breath. See it entering your body and visualize its nourishment. Imagine it going throughout your body, touching every nerve and cell. As you exhale, visualize the air leaving your body and carrying away any stress or anxiety. You may also visualize the breath taking earthly attachments with it as well. By adding visualization techniques, you can train your mind to focus on other things rather than the barrage of images and memories that come in such a chaotic fashion. Visualizing the breath will help keep you focused on your breath work as well. Keep in mind that you can visualize and focus on other things as well; many students visualize the Buddha seated beneath the Bodhi tree or choose a mandala to imagine. Another useful visualization technique is to focus on a candle's flame and then close your eyes and see the light's imprint in the darkness. Contemplating the nature of fire and light is quite thought-provoking and a beneficial exercise to be adept at.

With the added visualization to the breath work, you will notice that your mind has little room to distract you if you organize these techniques into a consistent rhythm. With the constant focus on breath and visualization, there will be very little distractions. Treat this session as the previous ones and take note of your experiences and perception.

Day Four

This session, we will add sound to our meditation. While you are welcome to find some meditation music online, we are going to focus on our own voices. There are plenty of mantras, or repeated statements to help concentration, that you find on the Internet, but we will simply use the word 'Om.' This sound is considered to be a primordial sound and is used in many mantras. With your breathing and visualization techniques in rhythm, we will add this sound to our session by saying it on our deep exhales. When you release this sound, be sure to draw out the 'o' sound as long as your exhale is. The sound should vibrate deep within your being and will be low in pitch and 'boomy.' This sound should be performed rather than simply said. If you are in a space where you need to be quiet, you can practice hearing this sound in your head, still letting it resonate throughout your entire being. By adding sound to our routine, along with the visualization and breath work, we find it to be easier to ignore the distractions of our minds.

If you choose to use music, make sure it is ambient or drone music that is long enough to be played throughout the session. If you wish to further this practice, you may find a suitable mantra or create one yourself that will benefit in reaching your goals. We now have a distinct set of techniques that busy all the senses: incense for smell, breath work for taste and touch, visualization for sight, sound for hearing, and also touch as you will feel the sound resonating. This arsenal of techniques is relatively basic, but it will be a firm foundation to start your meditation sessions. As you did with the previous days, take note of your experiences and be aware of your physical and emotional state.

Day Five

Now that we have a solid practice, we can implement it in our daily lives. This session will be very similar to Day Four, as we are using all of the techniques we've gathered in the previous days. For this session, you can add mudras, or hand gestures, to the practice. Pressing your hands together in a prayer formation or simply opening your palms to the world are considered mudras. There are many traditional mudras with a complex variety of symbolism for them. There are many books and resources online about these gestures, so for now, we will leave them out of this beginner's guide. From this point onward, you can customize the practice to suit your personal needs. Being aware of what works for you is very important for meditation. If you find that after several sessions some of these techniques hinder you in finding that meditative state, then discontinue doing them. From here, your practice will grow and become a natural and enjoyable routine. If you wish to lengthen your sessions, then do so, and keep in mind that you do not have to meditate every day and the routine doesn't have to be strictly followed. Consider doing your breath work at any moment if you feel stressed, or visualizing your chosen image throughout your day. Let meditation become a part of you in all aspects of life.

You now have a very solid stepping stone to continue moving down your newfound path of Buddhism. Keep in mind that this is a loose guideline. You can go at your own pace, and it doesn't have to be every day back-to-back. Let your meditation practice grow and evolve with you and always continue challenging yourself. Eventually, take time to add contemplation on the Four Noble Truths and concepts of the Eightfold Path to your practice to better align yourself with the Buddha and his wisdom. You may even visualize yourself as the content Buddha beneath the Bodhi tree. And as far as being able to tell if the meditation is benefitting you or not, you will know. You will feel the sensations of liberation grow within you, you will realize the truths of the self, and you will notice the difference in your perception of the world. Is this enlightenment? It's very hard to say, but always keep in mind that is doesn't matter if you become enlightened or not. If you do, will you even question it?

Chapter 10: Ritual, Prayer, and Offerings

Along with any religious or spiritual journey, you have certain actions and lifestyle choices that coincide with the doctrine. Assuming you aren't immediately becoming a monk, there are simple ways to incorporate Buddhism into your life besides meditational practices and familiarizing yourself with the history of the Buddha. Depending on the school and accepted practices, many Buddhists use ritual, prayer, and offerings to further their practice and enhance their ability to be compassionate and caring for other sentient beings. These practices mesh well with meditation, and depending on what you aim to achieve with your studies, you may wish to add them to your meditation sessions or daily life.

Ritual

Any action performed repetitively and within a pattern can be considered ritual, including your newfound meditational practice. Some people may consider their daily chores or preparation for work or school a ritual. But for our goals in this book, ritual is defined as religious ceremonies or actions that are organized according to a strict set of rules. With the information above, you have developed a meditation ritual and a ritual space as well. Within this space, you can add other ritual actions. Lighting of candles or incense, using your mantras, and the meditation itself all create a ritual designed to improve your practice. Adhering to your designated pattern will help increase the effectiveness of your ritual.

Within Buddhism, there are a handful of ritual actions that are adhered to: meditation, mantras, mudras, and pilgrimages make up the majority of popular ritual actions. By performing these actions repetitively, it is thought to align the student with their goals and create a powerful action that can liberate the practitioner and allow them to unlock the mysteries of reality.

There are many other ways of increasing the potency of your ritual as well: wearing a certain article of clothing when you meditate, using amulets and stones, meditating at sacred sites, and many other actions. The more complex or ancient the ritual is, it is thought, then the more powerful and useful it can be. As well as creating your own ritual, there are many ancient texts that lay out religious rituals and actions that are still practiced today.

Prayer

The act of trying to communicate with a spirit, deity, or any object of worship is ultimately prayer. This form of religious communication is found in all ancient cultures and acts as a mediator between Earth and other realms. Within Buddhism, mantras can be seen as a type of prayer. While Buddhism doesn't have a god to pray to, the concept of reducing the suffering of others can be seen to parallel prayer. Praying for someone to be healthy or live a righteous life is a powerful tool that is very useful for any spiritual path.

Although typically associated with communication to deities, prayer can be used to honor any figure worthy of praise or respect. By opening ourselves through prayer, we may find insight into many of the mysteries of life. This worship is often a form of expressing respect to the Buddha rather than deifying him like the Christian god or gods of ancient Greece. Within Buddhism, prayer is more akin to mantras and reverence rather than proper worship.

If you wish to add prayer to your practice, you can create a respectful and honorable phrase to meditate on or openly say during your practice. Simply thanking the Buddha for his insightful teachings is easy and powerful when combined with your other ritual practices.

Offerings

Symbolic gifts to deities or ancestors are found in all religions across the world. These offerings come in many forms and can be given at any time, but combined with your other ritual practices, these gifts make for very powerful symbolic gestures. In our Western society, we see offerings made to the dead in forms of flowers near gravestones. In all religions, offering gifts to the chosen god or honorable figure is considered to be very powerful, and often seen as a crucial sacrifice to prove your worthiness of the deities' attention.

Buddhism For Beginners

In Buddhism, since there is no god, the offerings are purely symbolic. It is effective in aligning you with the Buddha path, and also a selfless act as you give away valuable possessions in honor of Buddha. You can give popular offerings such as incense, candles, water, flowers, fruit, oils, and money, or you can get creative and offer a meal. Fasting can be seen as an offering as you are giving up food for the honorable figure. As we have discussed earlier, gaining karmic merit is of the utmost importance in Buddhism and giving offerings will add to your merit, helping to ensure a favorable rebirth in the next life.

Offerings can be given at any time, but there are also observed days where it is good to give offerings. Buddha's birthday, the Ghost Festival, and other holidays are celebrated within Buddhism as meaningful days where leaving offerings is particularly potent. Leaving offerings in your meditation space will add a nice aesthetic, and add to the ritual itself. Small bowls of fruit or water, lighting an incense with intention as an offering, and simply placing a penny in your space all work well as an offering. It is also helpful to have an altar or shelf specifically for offerings. You may also leave offerings outdoors, but be sure not to litter or leave anything harmful to animals or the environment.

With these added ceremonial actions, we can amplify the power of our meditational space and practices. By combining all of what we have learned in this book and adding to our daily lives, we will soon see the benefits of the Buddhist path. The compassion will grow inside you as you further your practice and stay dedicated to your path. With all these actions being performed, you transform your life and develop a respectable and powerful Buddhist practice. If you find that you need to further your practice even more as you progress, there are plenty of Buddhist temples and monasteries that are welcoming and have information for the adept as well as the beginner. Although most of you reading this will not choose a monastic lifestyle, the most devoted Buddhists choose to live at these monasteries, devoting their entire lives to the Buddhist path.

Chapter 11: Buddhism and Modern Life

With the technological advances of our society progressing rapidly, a lot of ancient knowledge gets left behind and replaced with science and materialism. The fast pace of our current world is overwhelming, and the idea of adding a Buddhist practice to an already busy schedule may seem out of reach. But these ancient practices and techniques are exactly what the world needs to balance out the intensity of the modern world. Although Buddhism can be complex and at times exhausting, it only takes a little bit of practice to make a world of difference in your life. Simply reading some Buddhist texts before bed or taking an extra 10 minutes of your day to breathe and relax, goes a long way in changing the stressful landscape that is our current world.

Buddhism For Beginners

It may seem like our society has no room or time for Buddhism, but in fact, this ancient philosophy is gaining more and more appreciation. The population is realizing that our technologies and lifestyles are having a detrimental effect on our minds. Addictions to phones and social media, abundant prescription pills, and unhealthy eating habits run rampant as we struggle to make ends meet and break the cycle of suffering. Never in history has the immense suffering of the earthly realm been so obvious, and this is why Buddhism is needed.

Even if you can't practice daily or devote your life to the Buddhist path, you can still use these techniques to reduce your suffering and the suffering of others. Even keeping the Buddhist concepts in your mind will help you remain balanced in the face of adversity, with or without a meditational practice.
Contemplation can be done anywhere at any time.

Buddhism For Beginners

Keeping balanced thoughts and clearing out the mind of clutter is key in surviving in this world, and not succumbing to the seemingly infinite number of stressors all around us.

Studies have proven that stress is very detrimental to the brain and body. How we deal with this stress is very important, and we can't simply suppress our stress with television and satisfying foods. These are impermanent solutions and bad habits that are being passed down to younger generations as we speak. By using the techniques described in this book, we can find a much healthier way to deal with our personal problems and the problems of our society.

By quieting the mind with meditation, we can detach from our stress and find a few moments of peace for even for a short while. These moments can do wonders to reverse the detrimental effects of stress, and scientific studies have proven this as well. Here, we see support from technology and science, which is an amazing breath of fresh air in the polluted sphere of modern life. The Buddha said that all suffering comes from ignorance, from the misunderstanding of reality. Science holds the potential to teach us about this reality and potentially aid Buddhism in reducing the suffering of all beings and breaking the cycle of samsara. If science can prove that meditation is healthy for the brain, then what else do these technologies hold? What can we achieve by taking the positive aspects of technological advances and combining them with Buddhist compassion? If the trend of using Buddhist techniques and philosophy to better our world continues, we may soon find out.

Although a truly enlightened experience may not be in our near future, or even in this life, we should not be discouraged from practicing the Buddhist methods. Even the slightest glimmer of liberation can be life-changing; even the slightest bit of compassion can change your day for the better or even change your life. We stand calmly before a manufactured world with the solution to our most terrifying problems inside our minds. If a simple act of compassion can improve our life, then what about a daily dedicated practice, or even group practices that can send a ripple throughout an entire city? It will not change overnight to free the world of suffering, and liberating all sentient beings will take many lifetimes. Hopefully, technology and science will work with the ancient philosophies to unite the world and show the population that Buddhism is worthwhile, even if practiced sparingly.

Buddhism boasts over 500 million followers worldwide. This number makes it the fourth most followed spiritual practice in the world. As time goes on, we will see science and Buddhism continuing to work together to reduce suffering. The Buddhist leader, His Holiness the Dalai Lama, has even spoke with curious scientists about our world's biggest problems. These scientists and His Holiness have started a healthy dialogue about the true nature of reality and how to unlock its mysteries. This open-mindedness that Buddhism holds is one of the main reasons the religion is so popular. By working with science and not against, it we move closer to breaking the cycle of death and rebirth, inching closer and closer to true liberation. The Dalai Lama has even stated in record that if science were to prove anything wrong about the Buddha's teaching, he would be willing to remove it from canon in Buddhist doctrine. Since Buddhism teaches that individuals vary greatly person to person, it is accepting of the variety of sects and schools within it. This is favored by Western psychologists and scientists as it does not contradict any of the ideas they attempt to prove.

Buddhism For Beginners

The Buddha's legacy melds well with 21st century science. Buddha was open to trying something, seeing if it's effective, then choosing to cherish or keep it in his life. This lack of blind faith that we see in the majority of other religions places Buddhism at the top of the list of most suitable spiritual studies for our modern society. If our population can cautiously approach science and Buddhism as two pieces of a universal puzzle, we may just be able to find peace and balance on Earth in the not so distant future. The despair and suffering of our world should be an eye-opening experience for generations to come. All the people who practice compassion, within the Buddhist sphere or not, are making a difference in this wicked cycle of life, and now, you the reader have the philosophy and spiritual technology to contribute to the liberation of all beings.

Conclusion

Thank you for making it through to the end of *Buddhism for Beginners: The Basic Understanding of Fundamental Buddhist Teachings, Concepts, and Practices.* Let's hope it was informative and able to provide you with all of the tools you need to achieve the goals you set out to do on your newfound Buddhist path.

The next step is to use this knowledge, practice these techniques, and share your experiences with your community. You may find other religions critiquing your studies or attempting to pull you away from your path, but always keep in mind that the open-mindedness of Buddhism is one of the keys to its success in the modern world. As you further your practice, do not hesitate to seek out other Buddhists and Buddhist-inspired literature to assist you on your path.

We have seen that the Eightfold Path and Four Noble truths can stand the test of time and the test of science. The Buddha was incredible in his teachings, but it's hard to say if he realized the profound impact he would have on the world. His main mission was to free the world of suffering by breaking the cycle of samsara, and it is safe to say that he has achieved his goal in some way. The teachings he shared with the world will last for many more millennia as it develops its relationship with science and truth seekers around the world. Regardless of the fracturing into individual schools and influence from cultures from around the world, Buddhism has held strongly to its ideals and mission. If we can truly transcend this earthly realm and see through the suffering, Buddhist philosophy is the path to this other worldly destination.

Buddhism For Beginners

As we conclude this book for beginners, I hope that you have found the methods and guidelines practical and easy to apply to your busy life. This path may start out rough as you begin to learn about the true nature of reality, but these realizations may shake the foundation of your life and lead you to places and people you could have never imagined. Stay true on your path and keep a keen eye on your goals. With all the wisdom shared by the Buddha, and through him in this book, it is highly recommended to, at the very least, take away this knowledge: Be compassionate, be selfless, and continue walking this path with fervor and respect.

Finally, if you found this book useful in any way, a review is always appreciated!

Garland P. Brackins

Buddhism For Beginners

Connect with us on our Facebook page www.facebook.com/bluesourceandfriends and stay tuned to our latest book promotions and free giveaways.

Made in the USA
Monee, IL
28 January 2021